FLAMINGOS

LIVING WILD

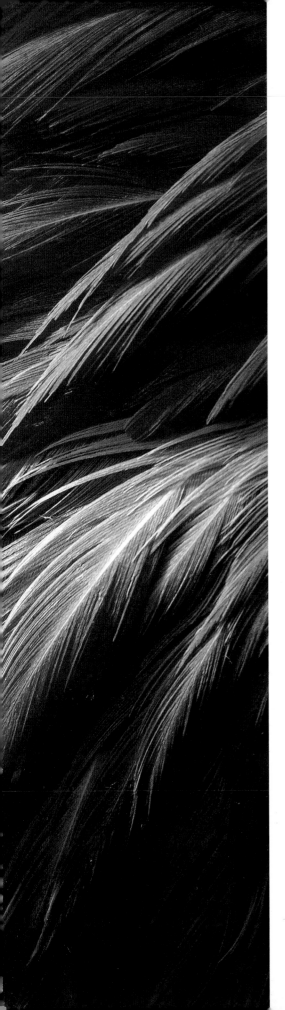

LIVING WILD

Published by Creative Paperbacks
P.O. Box 227, Mankato, Minnesota 56002
Creative Paperbacks is an imprint of The Creative Company
www.thecreativecompany.us

Design and production by Mary Herrmann
Art direction by Rita Marshall
Printed in the United States of America

Photographs by Alamy (James Brunker, Lebrecht Music and Arts Photo Library, Moviestore collection Ltd, Pictorial Press Ltd, Keren Su/China Span), Dreamstime (Galyna Andrushko, Bestshotsit, Lukas Blazek, Blufishdesign, Pierre Jean Durieu, Jakezc, Joasakura, Pedroec, Sunheyy, Attila Tatár), Getty Images (Martin Harvey), iStockphoto (AAR Studio, AKauroraPhotos, kaniwi, mjf99, Overlook, sdbower, sisoje, WLDavies), Shutterstock (anki21, Ian Cox, Kushch Dmitry, Steffen Foerster, Kacmerka, Alberto Loyo, Jeff McGraw, Fabien Monteil, Napat, Anna Omelchenko, komkrich ratchusiri, Styve Reineck, sevenke, Krzysztof Wiktor), SuperStock (John Warburton Lee, Minden Pictures), Wikipedia (Arpingstone, Robert Claypool, Foncea, Ghedoghedo, Iain and Sarah, Ltshears)

Library of Congress Cataloging-in-Publication Data
Gish, Melissa.
Flamingos / Melissa Gish.
p. cm. — (Living wild)
Includes bibliographical references and index.
Summary: A scientific look at flamingos, including their habitats, physical characteristics such as their coloration, behaviors, relationships with humans, and numbers of the tropical birds in the world today.
ISBN 978-1-60818-416-3 (hardcover)
ISBN 978-1-62832-002-2 (pbk)
1. Flamingos—Juvenile literature. I. Title. II. Series: Living wild.

QL696.C56G57 2014
598.3'5—dc23   2013031813

CCSS: RI.5.1, 2, 3, 8; RST.6-8.1, 2, 5, 6, 8; RH.6-8.3, 4, 5, 6, 7, 8

First Edition
9 8 7 6 5 4 3 2 1

FLAMINGOS

Melissa Gish

It is late spring at Kenya's Lake Nakuru National Park, and more than 2,000 lesser flamingos have arrived to join a colony numbering in the 100,000s.

It is late spring at Kenya's Lake Nakuru National Park, and more than 2,000 lesser flamingos have arrived to join a colony numbering in the 100,000s. For each bird, the time has come to select a mate, and with tens of thousands of individuals from which to choose, the choice is neither quick nor easy. Small groups form as the birds begin their mating dance by scurrying through the shallow water at the lake's edge.

Moving as one, they turn their heads to the left and then quickly to the right—repeating this motion as they zigzag through the water like a floating carpet of pink feathers. A female bird breaks away from the crowd. An interested male follows her. The two circle each other, bobbing their heads to signal their acceptance of the other. They will remain bonded with each other as they build a nest and raise a chick.

WHERE IN THE WORLD THEY LIVE

■ **Greater Flamingo**
Africa, southern
Europe, Middle East,
western India

■ **Lesser Flamingo**
sub-Saharan Africa,
western India

■ **American Flamingo**
Florida, Caribbean
islands, Galápagos,
Colombia to
Venezuela

■ **Andean Flamingo**
southern Peru,
Bolivia, northern
Chile, northwestern
Argentina

Divided into Old World and New World camps, the
six flamingo species are found primarily in Africa
and South America, with the three South American
species sharing much of their ranges. The colored dots
represent some common locations of all six of the
tropical water birds.

■ **Chilean Flamingo**
Peru, Bolivia, northern
Chile, northwestern
Argentina, Ecuador,
Brazil

■ **James's Flamingo**
southern Peru,
Bolivia, northern
Chile, northwestern
Argentina

PRETTY IN PINK

Flamingos are some of the most remarkable birds in the animal kingdom. They have the longest legs and longest necks in proportion to their body size of any bird, and they are among the most colorful large birds on the planet. Flamingos are the sole members of the genus *Phoenicopterus* (*FEE-nih-KOP-ter-uhs*). This name is Greek for "purple wing." The closest relatives of flamingos include storks, herons, egrets, ibises, and spoonbills—all large wading birds. Flamingos also share many characteristics with geese, such as the webbing between their toes and waterproof feathers. Like most birds, flamingos exhibit sexual dimorphism, which means males and females differ in appearance. In the case of flamingos, males are about one-third larger than their female counterparts.

The six flamingo species are divided into two general groups, Old World and New World, according to their general geographic location. The two Old World species, the greater flamingo and the lesser flamingo, are the largest and smallest species respectively. Greater flamingos weigh up to 9 pounds (4.1 kg) and have a wingspan

The roseate spoonbill's range extends from the Gulf Coast through the Caribbean to Chile and Argentina.

The scarlet ibis and roseate spoonbill, flamingo relatives, also feed on organisms that turn their feathers bright pink.

Flamingos spend a third of the day preening, or grooming and waterproofing their feathers with oil made by a gland near the tail.

of about 5.5 feet (1.7 m). Lesser flamingos average 3.5 pounds (1.6 kg) in weight and have a wingspan of slightly more than 3 feet (0.9 m). Old World flamingos are native to coastal areas of southern Europe, Africa, the Middle East, and western India.

There are four species of New World flamingos: American (or Caribbean), Andean, Chilean, and James's flamingos. Male American flamingos are the largest of the New World flamingos. They average six pounds (2.7 kg) in weight and have a wingspan of about five feet (1.5 m). American flamingos inhabit the Galápagos Islands and coasts and islands from Colombia to Venezuela as well as islands in the Caribbean Sea. Also, small flocks of American flamingos have been spotted in southern Florida's Everglades National Park—most likely they escaped from zoos or accidentally traveled to the United States from Cuba.

Andean flamingos are the only flamingos with bright yellow legs, as other flamingos typically have orange or pink coloration. They live in wetlands of the Andes Mountains in southern Peru, Bolivia, northern Chile, and northwestern Argentina. Chilean flamingos share the Andean flamingos' range but also extend into northern

American flamingo females are about 20 percent smaller than males, weighing almost 5 pounds (2.3 kg).

Chilean flamingos, at home in high-altitude places in South America, can withstand colder temperatures.

Peru, Ecuador, and western Brazil. Chilean flamingos have a characteristic red or pink ring around their ankle joints about halfway up the leg. (A flamingo's knees are actually hidden under its feathers near the top of the leg.) James's flamingos, also known as Puna flamingos, were named for British naturalist Harry Berkeley James, who first published information on this flamingo species in 1885. Only slightly larger than the lesser flamingo, the James's flamingo is the smallest of the New World flamingos. This flamingo also shares the Andean flamingo's range.

Like other birds, flamingos are warm-blooded, feathered, beaked animals that walk on two feet and lay eggs. Flamingos are tropical water birds that spend their lives in warm, muddy lagoons, **estuaries**, coastal wetlands, and shallow lakes—particularly seasonally occurring **soda lakes**. Flamingos are able to float on water and propel themselves forward by paddling with their webbed feet. However, they prefer to walk through shallow water and will typically fly over stretches of deep water rather than swim. The flamingo's long, flexible neck and spindly legs—up to 49 inches (124 cm) in length, depending on the species—allow this bird to feed in water that is often too deep for other kinds of water birds. All flamingos have three forward-pointing toes, but the greater, lesser, American, and Chilean flamingos also have one backward-pointing toe called a hallux. The flamingo stomps its webbed feet to stir up water, loosening food from the muddy bottom.

Flamingos feed with their heads upside down, holding their breath when submerged underwater. The flamingo's

The James's flamingo can be distinguished from other flamingo species by the yellow coloration on its bill.

Research at Kenya's Lake Bogoria in 2011 suggested that flamingos choose mates based on similar body language.

Some penguins and auks are filter feeders like flamingos, but only flamingos feed with their heads upside down.

bowl-shaped bill, which varies in its coloration pattern from species to species, is made of keratin, the same hard but flexible substance found in human fingernails. The lower jaw is attached to the flamingo's skull, while the upper jaw performs all the movement—this is unlike the jaw structure of most other birds. Flamingos feed on plant seeds as well as a variety of living creatures—algae, tiny fish, and **invertebrates**—by sifting these organisms from the water.

Rows of filtering plates are located on the edges of the upper and lower jaws. These plates, called lamellae, are shaped like combs with frayed edges, and they work like sieves. As the flamingo scoops up a mouthful of water, it loosely closes its bill. It then presses its fat, bristle-edged tongue against the roof of its mouth to force out the water through the lamellae, trapping the organisms inside its mouth. The flamingo performs this filtering action with great speed as it swings its head to and fro through the water or mud.

Greater, American, and Chilean flamingos have widely spaced filters for capturing seeds and prey such as worms, fish, insects, and mollusks up to one inch (2.5 cm) long. Pressing their tongue against the roof of their mouth 4 to 5

The number of lamellae in a flamingo's bill varies by species, from 13 per inch to more than 50 per inch.

A colony consisting of one million flamingos can consume roughly 200 tons (179 t) of algae per year.

times per second, they consume roughly 9.5 ounces (269 g) of food per day. Lesser, Andean, and James's flamingos have narrowly spaced filters designed to catch tiny flies, shrimp, and single-celled organisms such as algae and plankton. Their tongues move 20 times per second, filtering a little more than 2 ounces (56.7 g) of food per day.

The foods that flamingos eat are what give these birds their brilliant color. Algae and bacteria contain **pigments** called carotenoids, which give color to plants and animals. When flamingos eat carotenoid-producing organisms or other creatures, such as shrimp, that feed on these smaller organisms, the flamingos themselves become darker in color. Lesser flamingos, for example, are pale pink for most of the year, but when they feed on large amounts of carotenoid-rich algae during breeding season, their feathers, legs, and even eyes turn a brilliant crimson. Captive flamingos whose diets do not consist of carotenoid-rich foods will become paler in color, which is why most zoos today supplement flamingo diets with red algae. In the wild, the deep crimson American flamingos are the most colorful, while greater flamingos are naturally the palest pink.

Flamingos sometimes feed on microscopic organisms called thermophiles, which thrive in hot springs.

Mountain-dwelling flamingos survive overnight temperatures as low as -22 °F (-30 °C) by gathering near hot springs.

Flamingos feed on blue-green algae called cyanobacteria that grows abundantly in mineral-rich Lake Bogoria.

BIRDS OF A FEATHER

Because flamingos are lightweight birds that spend most of their time on the ground, they are vulnerable to predators. To help protect themselves, they live in flocks that may number from several hundred to several thousand. Flamingos inhabit places that most other animals find inhospitable because of the harsh extremes. They visit mangrove swamps, estuaries, and intertidal zones (ocean shore areas that are underwater at high tide but exposed at low tide). The water in these habitats may be very fresh if rainfall is consistent or very salty if it is infrequent. Nevertheless, such areas are rich in the nutrients that tiny organisms need to flourish. The most productive aquatic environments on Earth are soda lakes, which explode seasonally with protein-rich algae, insects, brine shrimp, and other tiny creatures brought on by heavy spring rains.

Flamingos do not **migrate** seasonally, but they typically move from place to place throughout the year in search of food and nest sites. Flamingo flocks join together to form enormous colonies at soda lakes in South America or Africa, where they feast in preparation for the task

To conserve heat, flamingos bend their necks—usually to the right—and tuck their heads into the feathers on their backs.

In 2010, flamingos were seen smearing extra oil on their feathers to darken their color during mating season.

Flamingos communicate using a variety of sounds, including grunting and growling as well as honking like geese.

of breeding and raising chicks. In the heat of summer, as water **evaporates** from a soda lake, a thick crust of minerals is left to bake in the sun, forming a hard salt flat. The world's largest salt flat is Salar de Uyuni in Bolivia. This area of approximately 4,085 square miles (10,580 sq km) is situated in the Andes Mountains at about 12,000 feet (3,658 m) above sea level. Tens of thousands of flamingos go there to breed and raise chicks during the summer, returning to warmer, lower-altitude habitats in winter. In Africa, flamingos gather at six or seven different soda lakes in the Great Rift Valley. Northern Tanzania's Lake Natron attracts nearly 2 million lesser flamingos to its salt islands, which form in the center of water so rich in algae containing red pigments that the water appears redder than flamingo feathers.

Flamingos of all ages gather together during breeding season, but they do not begin to reproduce until they are about six years old. If food is not abundant, flamingos may not reproduce at all in a given year, but if conditions are favorable, breeding occurs among most eligible members of a colony. Flamingos attempt to impress potential mates by participating in an assortment of synchronized

movements called courtship displays. The type of display varies by species but includes activities such as marching, head flagging, wing saluting, and leg-wing stretching, and all are performed in unison. When marching, flamingos bunch together as closely as possible and move in one direction; then they suddenly turn and move in another direction. Similarly grouped tightly together, flamingos perform head flagging by stretching their necks and lifting their bills upward as high as they can. They then swing their heads from the right to the left and back again in rapid harmony. Wing saluting is performed by repeatedly stretching the neck forward, raising the tail,

Flamingo mates communicate constantly from the nest-building stage until their young hatch.

Stress or illness may cause flamingos to abandon their chicks, which are sometimes adopted by birds without offspring.

and outstretching the wings for a few seconds. Flamingos also extend one leg straight back at the same time as they stretch one wing straight back in leg-wing stretching.

Flamingos form pair bonds that last through a breeding season. Together, the two flamingos use their bills to scrape up a tower of salt and mud with a shallow bowl in the center. The sun bakes this structure, which can stand as high as 24 inches (61 cm), to rock-hard strength. Pairs spend up to six weeks bonding and nest building. Then a single chalky-white egg, about twice as big as a chicken egg, is laid. The tower protects the egg from a flood, which sometimes occurs if the salt flat cracks, and keeps the egg cooler than if it were laid directly on the ground. The parents take turns sitting on or standing over the egg, incubating it for 27 to 31 days and gently turning it daily.

Using its **egg tooth**, the chick chips through the hard shell of its egg. This may take between 24 and 36 hours, during which time the chick cheeps constantly, and the parents answer in order to establish a voice bond that will allow them to recognize each other later. Parents will feed only their own chick. Newly hatched chicks weigh between two and three ounces (56.7–85 g). They are covered with fluffy gray or white **down**, and their bills are straight and red. Chicks are weak and fragile, but they can lift their heads long enough to be fed crop milk by their parents. Crop milk is a red liquid secreted by glands in the adult flamingo's throat. It is 9 percent protein and 15 percent fat, and it contains some of the adult's own red and white blood cells. Chicks eat crop milk for two months as the filter system in their bills develops.

Week-old chicks wander from their nests and gather in groups called crèches. Here they find relative safety in numbers. At about 11 weeks old, chicks start to grow

Juvenile flamingos find safety in numbers before developing flight feathers, as they can only try to outrun predators.

A marabou stork has a pouch on its throat that may be used for courtship displays rather than storing food.

flight feathers, and their bills begin to curve. Juvenile flamingos remain gray or white until they reach two or three years of age, when their feathers turn pink.

Both adult and young flamingos are threatened by a variety of predators. However, chicks and eggs are particularly vulnerable, since flamingos do not have the body strength or bill design to fend off attackers and protect their young. In South America and the Bahamas, foxes, wild cats, eagles, hawks, **feral** pigs, and snakes attack flamingos and raid their nests. Leopards, cheetahs, jackals, and baboons regularly attack adult Old World flamingos, while hyenas, warthogs, mongooses, and wild dogs typically target eggs and chicks.

More threatening to Old World flamingos than any of these other predators, though, is the marabou stork, also called the undertaker stork because of its long, black coat of feathers and nearly bald head. Just a few of these 20-pound (9.1 kg) birds with their thick, sharp, 14-inch-long (35.6 cm) bills can kill hundreds of flamingo chicks in a matter of hours. As devastating as this may seem, in a typical colony of 500,000 lesser flamingos on an African lake, the **mortality rate** of chicks may be as low as 5 percent.

Flamingos have 19 neck bones, called cervical vertebrae, which allow the neck to twist and bend.

For thousands of years, Asian art has featured a variety of large birds such as flamingos and cranes.

SOULS OF THE SUN

The flamingo has been part of the **mythology** and legends of many **cultures** for thousands of years. In ancient Egypt, the flamingo signified the color red, and Egyptian mythology explained that when a holy tree burst into flames, the sun god Ra emerged from the fire as the Bennu, a brilliant crimson-colored bird. The flamingo, which once lived in great numbers along the Nile River, became the living embodiment of the Bennu, and this bird was believed to carry the soul of Ra. In the town of Naqada, on the western bank of the Nile, **archaeologists** discovered images of flamingos painted on pottery that is more than 3,200 years old.

The story of the Bennu perhaps gave rise to the Greek myth of the phoenix in the fifth century B.C. Every 1,000 years, this bird would burn itself and be reborn from the ashes. Similar mythical birds can be found in symbolic tales of transformation the world over, from the Iranian huma to the Slavic firebird.

When the Romans visited Egypt in the first century B.C., they captured flamingos and served the birds' tongues to royalty. In the North African country of

Flamenco is a Spanish dance that is said to resemble the quick movements of flamingos performing courtship displays.

Since 1589, flamingo costumes have been a tradition at the annual Fiesta de Chutillos in Potosí, Bolivia.

The estimated life span of a wild flamingo is 20 to 30 years, as captive flamingos typically live more than 30 years.

Tunisia, flamingo meat was still considered a delicacy hundreds of years later. At an archaeological site in El-Djem that dates to the third century A.D., **mosaic** artwork was found depicting a flamingo being prepared for cooking. Around the same time, flamingos were also kept as pets and displayed in traveling circuses and private zoos. On the island of Sicily, another mosaic was found—this one dating to the fourth century A.D.—of a child's chariot being pulled by red flamingos.

In the Americas, the Moche civilization arose about 2,000 years ago in northwestern Peru. The Moche often depicted animals and birds—including flamingos—in their art and pottery. In 1987, Peruvian archaeologist Walter Alva discovered a tomb of a Moche king dating to the second century A.D. Among the artifacts found there were ornaments and headdresses made of flamingo feathers.

While flamingos are no longer widely worshiped as gods or magical beasts, they are still greatly admired for their beauty and grace. Flamingos are a mainstay of zoos around the world, but an Australian ban on exotic bird importation has left two specimens as the sole captive flamingos on the entire continent—and they also

happen to be the oldest flamingos in the world. A greater flamingo, nicknamed "Greater," arrived at the Adelaide Zoo in 1933 and is thought to be more than 80 years old. A Chilean flamingo arrived in 1948, just prior to the ban. The two flamingos display no fear of people despite an incident in 2008, when four teenagers attacked Greater, fracturing his skull and blinding him in one eye. After a year of medical treatments and therapy, Greater recovered and returned to his zoo home, taking up his familiar post beside his enclosure partner of more than 50 years.

In America, flamingos have often been viewed as comedic, showy characters. People who share such traits as long legs are sometimes associated with the birds.

Genetic differences prevent the various flamingo species from breeding with one another.

Standing out against its glass and steel surroundings, the color of Chicago's Flamingo sculpture is known as "Calder red."

Infamous New York gangster Benjamin "Bugsy" Siegel had a girlfriend named Virginia Hill, who had long, skinny legs, so Siegel called her "Flamingo." In 1945, Siegel went to Las Vegas to build a casino—the biggest, fanciest casino anyone had ever built at the time. He spent $6 million on the lavish building—and he named it the Flamingo in Virginia's honor. Today, the Flamingo Las Vegas, which still features tropical décor and a garden courtyard that is home to a flock of live Chilean flamingos, is the oldest casino in operation on the Las Vegas Strip.

A troupe of comical flamingos with super-skinny legs appears in the Disney film *Fantasia 2000*. The birds struggle to keep one member of the troupe in step, but he's too busy playing with a yo-yo—and entangling his fellow flamingos—to follow his dance routine. Known as Yo-Yo Flamingo, the character also appeared in several episodes of *House of Mouse*, a Disney television series from the early 2000s. Another flamingo entertainer was Placido Flamingo, a *Sesame Street* character modeled after Spanish opera singer Plácido Domingo. The singing bird appeared at the Nestopolitan Opera, a fictional venue created to introduce classical music to *Sesame Street* viewers. Real

Yo-Yo Flamingo's obsession makes him stand out from the crowd and gets everyone in a jumble.

In 1973, American artist Alexander Calder created the 50-ton (45.4 t) steel *Flamingo* for the plaza of Chicago's Kluczynski Federal Building.

Don Featherstone modeled his first plastic flamingos after a National Geographic magazine's photographs.

In the Hindu tradition, Brahma, the four-armed, four-faced god of creation, is depicted riding a brilliant red flamingo.

flamingos are the stars of Disneynature's 2008 film *The Crimson Wing: Mystery of the Flamingos*, which tells the story of a colony of nesting flamingos on a salt island in the Great Rift Valley's Lake Natron.

In fictional books, flamingo characters often find themselves standing out from other kinds of birds. Jill Ker Conway's 2006 book *Felipe the Flamingo* tells of a young flamingo who is left behind when his flock migrates. Other birds adopt him until his family returns. And in *Sylvie* (2009), by Jennifer Sattler, a young flamingo begins experimenting with foods that change her pink coloration. Jamie Harper's book *Miss Mingo and the First Day of School* (2009) presents a flamingo teacher getting to know her students.

Perhaps the most familiar flamingos of all are the plastic lawn flamingos. First designed in 1957 by Don Featherstone for a Massachusetts plastics company, the pink lawn ornaments have become so widely known that they have inspired characters in film. In the 2011 animated movie *Gnomeo and Juliet*, two love-struck lawn gnomes make friends with a lonely plastic flamingo named Featherstone. In 1987, "Pink Floyd" the Chilean flamingo

Featherstone the lawn flamingo helps bring Gnomeo and Juliet closer together as they hide from their fighting families.

escaped from Tracy Aviary in Salt Lake City, Utah, and took up residence at the Great Salt Lake. City officials planted a flock of plastic pink flamingos around the lake to help Pink Floyd feel less lonely, which appeared to work, since the bird continued to live at the lake until 2005.

Since 2002, original Featherstone-designed lawn flamingos have been available online through GetFlocked .com. In 2004, the company sent a box of flamingos to American soldiers in Iraq to remind them of their homes and neighborhoods. The soldiers wrote back, expressing their delight at the surprise, saying, "your birds have brought nothing but smiles to the people who see them.... They are pure Americana."

FROM *ALICE IN WONDERLAND*

"Get to your places!" shouted the Queen in a voice of thunder, and people began running about in all directions, tumbling up against each other; however, they got settled down in a minute or two, and the game began. Alice thought she had never seen such a curious croquet-ground in her life; it was all ridges and furrows; the balls were live hedgehogs, the mallets live flamingoes, and the soldiers had to double themselves up and to stand on their hands and feet, to make the arches.

The chief difficulty Alice found at first was in managing her flamingo: she succeeded in getting its body tucked away, comfortably enough, under her arm, with its legs hanging down, but generally, just as she had got its neck nicely straightened out, and was going to give the hedgehog a blow with its head, it would twist itself round and look up in her face, with such a puzzled expression that she could not help bursting out laughing: and when she had got its head down, and was going to begin again, it was very provoking to find that the hedgehog had unrolled itself, and was in the act of crawling away: besides all this, there was generally a ridge or furrow in the way wherever she wanted to send the hedgehog to, and, as the doubled-up soldiers were always getting up and walking off to other parts of the ground, Alice soon came to the conclusion that it was a very difficult game indeed.

by Lewis Carroll (1832-98)

PLEASE PASS THE SALT

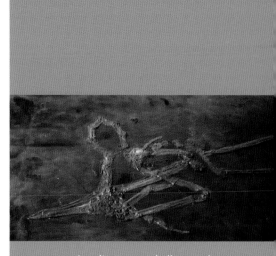

Juncitarsus merkeli *was a large flamingo relative that lived about 40 million years ago.*

The first flamingo ancestor most closely related to modern flamingos was *Phoenicopterus croizeti*, which lived about 40 million years ago. This robust bird was one of the first birds to wade and feed in shallow water but, unlike modern flamingos, was ill-equipped for distance flying. Fossils of it have been found in France. Another flamingo ancestor shared prehistoric wetland and rainforest habitats of central Australia with many other bird species as well as early crocodiles about 25 million years ago. Standing about five feet (1.5 m) tall, *Phoeniconotius eyrensis* was one of the largest flamingo ancestors ever discovered. Flamingos disappeared from Australia millions of years ago as climate change caused much of their habitat to dry up and turn to desert. Many fossils of early flamingos and other wading birds have been found in the province of South Australia at Lake Eyre, a shallow salt flat with sparse seasonal water.

On the other side of the world, one of the smallest and most recent flamingo ancestors existed in North America until the last glacial period ended about 11,000 years ago. Fossilized remains of *Phoenicopterus minutus*, whose name

Of Salar de Uyuni's 11 billion tons (10 billion t) of salt, less than 28,000 tons (25,000 t) is mined each year.

Flamingos seek out lakes in which few or no fish live because fish compete for the flamingos' favorite food: algae.

means "little flamingo," were first found in California's Mojave Desert in the 1950s. Long ago, North America's flamingos were forced to move toward the equator, where they continued to **evolve** into the modern species living on Earth today.

Flamingos are uniquely suited to their shallow-water environments, which is why scientists and conservationists are concerned about these birds' future on the planet. Flamingo habitats are being disturbed and even transformed by industry, particularly by the mining of sodium carbonate, the salty mineral present in the very lakes where flamingos feed and nest. Dozens of studies are being conducted in countries containing flamingo habitats—including Afghanistan, Argentina, India, Kenya, Siberia, Tanzania, and Turkey—to determine how mining might affect flamingo breeding and survival.

Sodium carbonate is used in a variety of products, from glass to detergent to toothpaste, and it is even used as a food additive to keep powdery foods such as cocoa mix and dry oatmeal from caking. To extract this chemical from soda lakes, water is pumped into enclosed pits and allowed to evaporate. The remaining salty residue hardens

in the sun and is then cut into blocks. Taking water from the lakes in this way speeds up the lakes' own evaporation process, leaving flamingos with less water for feeding and fewer salt islands for nesting and raising young. In addition, the human activities disturb flamingos, who may then avoid breeding grounds altogether.

Scientists are particularly alarmed at the Tanzanian government's approval of a major soda mining operation on Lake Natron, where 65 to 75 percent of the world's lesser flamingo population nests each year. Continued mining in Africa could not only decimate flamingo populations, but it could also affect the lives of the people in mining nations.

The flamingo's 12 principal flight feathers, which are black, are visible only when the wings are extended.

Flamingos thrive in the heat at Lake Natron, where temperatures can reach 120 °F (48.9 °C).

For example, thousands of people visit Lake Natron each year to see the flamingos, providing the Tanzanian people with tourism dollars. While soda mining may be profitable in the short term, the soda supply will not last forever. Without flamingos to draw tourists year after year, the Tanzanian economy will suffer.

Industrialists believe the populations of roughly 2.2 to 3.2 million lesser flamingos and 550,000 greater flamingos are stable, yet flamingos are part of a delicate ecosystem that is being altered, leading to a persistent annual decline in flamingo numbers. Populations of New World flamingos, which are already smaller (with James's flamingos numbering about 64,000 and Andean flamingos fewer than 34,000), face similar challenges. In South America, mining operations and crop irrigation deplete water from many flamingo habitats. As cities expand, the building of roads and pollution from sewage also contribute to habitat destruction. In addition, thousands of flamingo eggs are collected—even from protected areas—to be illegally sold for food, and flamingos can fall victim to **poaching** for their oil and feathers, materials that many **indigenous** people believe can prevent and cure a variety of health problems. The population of roughly 200,000 Chilean flamingos is affected by tourists and photographers as well, whose interference often leads to nest abandonment.

In North America, decades of overhunting and habitat destruction in the early 20th century led to a sharp decline in American flamingo populations, and by the mid-20th century, fewer than 22,000 of these birds remained. However, conservation efforts, including the establishment of wildlife reserves, enabled the flamingos to mount a strong comeback. The population of American flamingos today is estimated to be roughly 850,000.

Although their numbers continue to decline,

James's flamingos were believed extinct until a small group was found in 1956 and protection measures helped them recover.

Flamingos need to get a running start of several strides to lift their bodies off the ground for flight.

Flamingos can reach speeds of up to 35 miles (56.3 km) per hour when flying long distances in flocks.

government-sponsored protected areas offer some support for the other three species of New World flamingos. One of the most valuable flamingo habitats in South America is the Eduardo Avaroa Andean Fauna National Reserve in southwestern Bolivia, which covers more than 1.7 million acres (687,966 ha). The Salinas and Aguada Blanca Natural Reserve in Peru also provides protected nesting grounds high in the Andes Mountains. Los Flamencos National Reserve in Chile is another important flamingo habitat. The reserve's major lake, Salar de Tara (Tara Salt Flat) was designated a Wetland of International Importance in 1996 by the Ramsar Convention, an international treaty for the conservation of wetlands. In addition to protecting flamingos, the site also offers sanctuary to many of the flamingo's high-altitude neighbors, including the Andean goose; the tall, flightless Darwin's rhea; and the quail-like puna tinamou.

Park rangers patrol flamingo nest sites to offer protection from poachers, and researchers continue to monitor flamingo populations. As of 2013, Argentina, Bolivia, and Chile were working to create a tri-national reserve to provide even more protected flamingo habitat.

While such measures are positive developments, both human interference and climate change persist in affecting flamingo behavior and mortality around the world. Flamingos have **adapted** to their harsh environments over countless generations. Forcing these birds to adapt further to even more challenging conditions as a result of human activities seriously imperils their ability to survive and thrive. Conducting further research and strengthening conservation measures will be necessary steps to take to save flamingos from an uncertain future.

Flamingos have been known to travel more than 370 miles (595 km) in a single night between habitats.

ANIMAL TALE: THE TEARS OF THE GODDESS

In South America, birds are important creatures in many mythical stories that explain how things came to be. Drawn from Argentinean folklore, the following story gives an account for the presence of salt in Argentina's largest naturally occurring salt lake, Mar Chiquita, which means "little sea" in Spanish, and tells how the flamingos came to inhabit the lake's shallow edges and muddy islands.

Long ago, a water goddess lived in a palace near a freshwater pond that was surrounded by a beautiful forest. A small band of warriors watched over the land, welcoming anyone to gather berries in the forest and catch fish in the pond. One day, a tribe of men invaded the peaceful land.

The leader of the invaders went to the palace and told the goddess, "We claim this land for ourselves and will strike down your guardsmen unless you surrender."

"I cannot give you the land," replied the goddess. "It is for everyone to share equally."

Upon hearing this response, the invaders attacked. The goddess's guardsmen were strong and fought well, but the invaders were equally powerful. Day after day, night after night, the battle raged on, with neither side gaining any ground over the other.

Once again, the leader of the invading tribe went to the goddess. "How long can you stand against us?" he asked. "We will not give up. Give us your land."

"I will not," persisted the goddess. "All must share the land."

This refusal angered the warrior, who raged, "If we cannot possess this land for ourselves, then no one shall have it."

Furiously and selfishly, the warrior ordered his

men to burn the beautiful forest and kill or drive away the animals. The men threw wide nets into the pond and pulled out all the fish, leaving them to die in the sun. Through all of this, the goddess stood in her tower, watching her guardsmen try but fail to stop the rampage, and she felt great sadness. She began to cry. For three days, the madness continued—fires burning, trees falling, animals dying—and the goddess cried.

Her sad, heavy breath stirred the air and brought a great storm to the land. The wind blew the smoke in gusts, blinding the attackers as well as her own guardsmen. All the men gasped for air and, finding none, died. Then the goddess's salty tears poured down her palace walls and flooded the land. The salt water put out the fires, but it was too late. Everything and everyone in the land was dead.

And then the smoke cleared, and the water settled. In place of the forest stretched a great, salty lake. Its shores were black mud and stubbles of scorched grass. The bodies of the goddess's guardsmen floated in the water.

Then the goddess smiled and blew a soft, warm breath over the land. Suddenly, new marsh grass began to sprout. Algae began to bloom in the water, and tiny shrimp fluttered to life. And the goddess's guardsmen transformed into birds, their wounds healing in brilliant pink streaks. They became flamingos, and to this day, they gather in great numbers at the shores of the salt lake to guard the goddess's palace, now hidden beneath the salty waters of Mar Chiquita, surrounded by simple grassland that no one would ever wish to possess again.

GLOSSARY

adapted – changed to improve its chances of survival in its environment

archaeologists – people who study human history by examining ancient peoples and their artifacts

cultures – particular groups in a society that share behaviors and characteristics that are accepted as normal by that group

down – small feathers whose barbs do not interlock to form a flat surface, thus giving a fluffy appearance

egg tooth – a hard, toothlike tip of a young bird's beak or a young reptile's mouth, used only for breaking through its egg

estuaries – the mouths of large rivers, where the tides (from oceans or seas) meet the streams

evaporates – changes from liquid to invisible vapor, or gas

evolve – to gradually develop into a new form

feral – in a wild state after having been domesticated

gland – an organ that produces chemical substances used by other parts of the body

indigenous – originating in a particular region or country

invertebrates – animals that lack a backbone, including shellfish, insects, and worms

migrate – to undertake a regular, seasonal journey from one place to another and then back again

mortality rate – the number of deaths in a certain area or period

mosaic – a picture or design made by arranging small pieces of colored material such as glass, stone, or tile

mythology – a collection of myths, or popular, traditional beliefs or stories that explain how something came to be or that are associated with a person or object

nutrients – substances that give an animal energy and help it grow

pigments – materials or substances present in the tissues of animals or plants that give them their natural coloring

poaching – hunting protected species of wild animals, even though doing so is against the law

soda lakes – lakes characterized by heavy concentrations of salt and related chemicals

SELECTED BIBLIOGRAPHY

Aeberhard, Matthew, and Leander Ward. *The Crimson Wing: Mystery of the Flamingos*. DVD. Paris, France: Disneynature, 2008.

Collar, Nigel. *Pink Flamingos*. New York: Abbeville Press, 2000.

Flamingo Resource Centre. "Flamingo Basics." http://www.flamingoresources.org/basics.html.

McMillan, Bruce. *Wild Flamingos*. Boston: Houghton Mifflin, 1997.

San Diego Zoo. "San Diego Zoo Animals: Flamingo." http://animals.sandiegozoo.org/animals/flamingo.

SeaWorld Education Department. Flamingos. http://www.seaworld.org/animal-info/info-books/flamingo/pdf/ib-flamingo.pdf. SeaWorld, 2005.

Note: Every effort has been made to ensure that any websites listed above were active at the time of publication. However, because of the nature of the Internet, it is impossible to guarantee that these sites will remain active indefinitely or that their contents will not be altered.

Flamingos use their excellent vision
and hearing to stay in contact with
other members of their flock.

INDEX

activities 12, 15, 37, 42
  flying 15, 37, 42
  preening 12
  walking 15

chicks 8, 22, 25–26
  appearance at birth 25
  food sources 25
  mortality rate 26

conservation efforts 41, 42, 43
  Ramsar Convention 42
  wildlife reserves 41, 42

cultural influences 29–31, 33–35, 44
  artwork 30, 33
  entertainment 33–34
  folklore 44
  food 29–30
  lawn ornaments 34–35
  literature 34
  mythologies 29
  pets 30
  religion 30, 34
  symbolism 29

eggs 15, 24–25, 26, 41

food 15, 16, 19, 21, 22, 38
  algae 16, 19, 21, 22, 38
  fish 16, 38
  insects 16, 19, 21
  mollusks 16
  seeds 16
  shrimp 19, 21
  worms 16

habitats 7, 10, 12, 14, 15, 19, 21–22, 26, 30, 31, 33, 34, 35,
      37, 38, 39–40, 41, 42, 44
  Africa 7, 10, 12, 21, 22, 26, 29, 30, 38, 39–40
    individual countries 7, 30, 38, 39–40
  Asia 38
  Australia 30, 31, 37
  estuaries 15, 21
  Europe 10, 12, 30, 37
  islands 12, 22, 34, 39, 44
  lagoons 15
  loss of 41
  mountains 12, 19, 42
  North America 10, 12, 31, 33, 35, 37, 38, 41
    U.S. 10, 12, 31, 33, 35, 38
  soda lakes 15, 21–22, 26, 38
  South America 10, 12, 14, 21, 22, 26, 30, 38, 41, 42, 44
    individual countries 10, 12, 14, 30, 38, 42, 44
  wetlands 12, 15, 37, 44

life expectancy 30–31

mating 7–8, 15, 22–24, 29, 38
  courtship displays 23, 29

migration 21, 34

national parks 7, 12

nests 21, 24, 25, 26, 38, 39, 41, 42
  abandonment of 41

New World flamingos, 10, 11, 12, 14–15, 16, 19, 31, 33, 34,
      40–41, 42
  American flamingos 10, 12, 15, 16, 19, 41
  Andean flamingos 10, 12, 15, 19, 41
  Chilean flamingos 10, 12, 14, 15, 16, 19, 31, 33, 34, 41
  James's flamingos 10, 12, 14–15, 19, 40–41

Old World flamingos 7, 10, 11–12, 14, 15, 16, 19, 26, 31, 39, 40
  greater flamingos 10, 11, 15, 16, 31, 40
  lesser flamingos 7, 10, 11, 12, 14, 15, 19, 26, 39, 40

Phoenicopterus genus 11

physical characteristics 8, 11, 12, 14–15, 16, 19, 21, 22, 23,
      24, 25, 26, 30, 31, 37, 41
  bills 15, 16, 23, 24, 25, 26
  color 11, 12, 14, 16, 19, 26
  egg tooth 25
  eyes 19
  feathers 8, 11, 12, 14, 15, 19, 21, 22, 26, 30, 31, 41
  feet 11, 15
  legs 11, 12, 14, 15, 19, 24
  necks 11, 15, 21, 23
  sizes 11, 12, 14–15, 21, 25, 37

populations 39, 40–42

predators 21, 26

relatives 11, 22, 37
  ancestors 37
  geese 11, 22
  wading birds 11

scientific studies 15, 38

social behaviors 7, 21, 22, 25, 26, 42
  in colonies 7, 21, 22, 26
  communication 22
  in crèches 25
  in flocks 21, 42

speed 42

threats 31, 37, 38–41, 43
  climate change 37, 43
  human interference 31, 41, 43
  overhunting 41
  poaching 41
  soda mining 38–41

zoos 12, 19, 30, 31